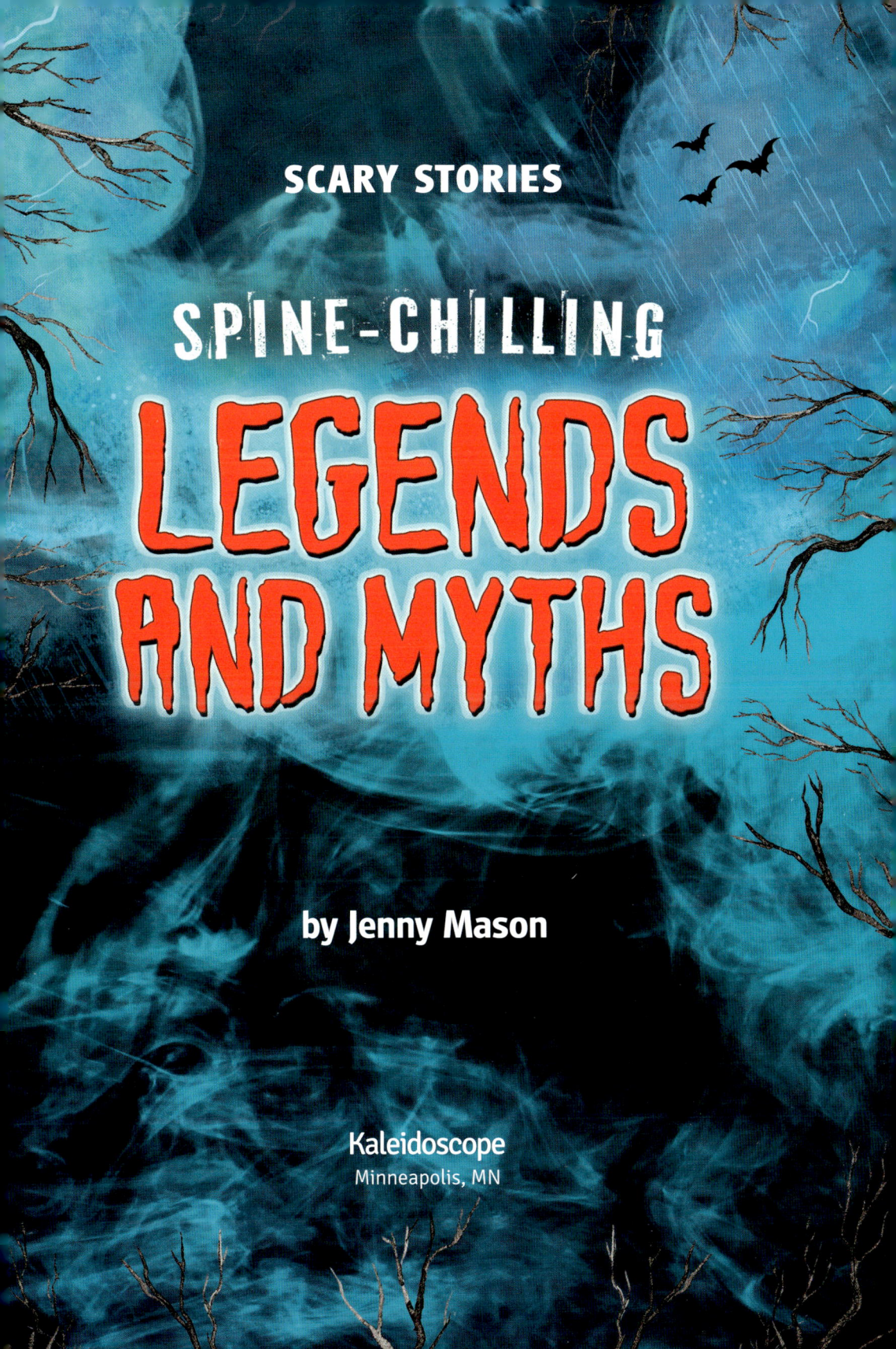

# SCARY STORIES

# SPINE-CHILLING LEGENDS AND MYTHS

by Jenny Mason

Kaleidoscope
Minneapolis, MN

## The Quest for Discovery Never Ends

..............................................

This edition first published in 2025 by Kaleidoscope Publishing, Inc.

No part of this publication may be reproduced in whole or in part without written permission of the publisher.

For information regarding permission, write to
Kaleidoscope Publishing, Inc.
6012 Blue Circle Drive
Minnetonka, MN 55343

Library of Congress Control Number
2024935455

ISBN
978-1-64519-838-3 (library bound)
978-164519-886-4 (ebook)

Text copyright © 2025 by Kaleidoscope Publishing, Inc. All-Star Sports, Bigfoot Books, and associated logos are trademarks and/or registered trademarks of Kaleidoscope Publishing, Inc.

Developed and produced by Focus Strategic Communications Inc.

Printed in the United States of America.

**FIND ME IF YOU CAN!**

Bigfoot lurks within one of the images in this book. It's up to you to find him!

# TABLE OF CONTENTS

Beware .................................................. 4
Nightmare Island ................................. 6
In the Forbidden Forest ..................... 14
A Deadly Ride ..................................... 22
Beyond the Book ................................ 28
Research Ninja ................................... 29
Further Resources ............................. 30
Glossary .............................................. 31
Index .................................................... 32
Photo Credits ..................................... 32
About the Author ............................... 32

# BEWARE

There's no escape. Ghosts, demons, and spirits are everywhere. Travel anywhere in the world. You will find them. Travel back in time. They'll be waiting there. They are part of humankind's **myths**. Those are the ancient stories people tell to explain the unknown. How did the world begin? Why are we here? Why do we die?

## FREAKY FACT

15% of the world's population believes in ghosts. That is one in every 6 people.

Some ghosts emerge from real events. That makes them the stuff of **legends**. Legends are repeated over and over. They carry ghosts forever into the future. So, you see, there really is no escape. Not from an island of haunted dolls. Not from a nightmare forest that traps people in a time net. Not from a highway ghost that lures drivers off the road. Get ready for goosebumps.

# NIGHTMARE ISLAND

Whispers prickle through the air. Water laps at the island shore. Little bodies hang from every tree. Dozens of them wrap around tree trunks. They dangle from branches. Dirt cakes their chubby cheeks. Some have glassy eyes half opened. Others are missing their eyes. They stare through black holes.

*Tap, tap, tap, tap*. Don Julian Santana Barrera hammers a nail through a doll's arm. Once it is fixed to the tree, he moves on. There are more dolls to hang throughout the island. He cannot stop. This **ritual** is the only way to please the ghost that haunts him.

Nobody knows why Don Julian ran away from his family in the 1950s. He traveled to Teshuilo Lake in Mexico City and made his new home on a small island. One day, Don Julian found the body of a little girl. She had drowned.

Santa Muerte represents death in Mexican folklore.

    The girl's spirit haunted the island. Don Julian heard soft crying and whispers at night. According to Mexico's ancient myths, death can happen twice. First your body dies. That is natural. If you are forgotten, then your spirit or ghost dies. That death is terrible. Don Julian would not let the girl die twice.

Don Julian hung one doll to make the spirit happy. This act quieted the spirit for a while. Whenever it reappeared, he hung another doll. He dug through dumpsters to find more dolls. Sometimes he pulled them from the canal.

Over time, the island became called the Island of Dolls. Sometimes tourists hang new dolls. Some say they hear the dolls whispering to each other. Rumors claim the dolls move at night. Haunted or not, maybe the dolls help people remember Don Julian's spirit.

**CREEPY QUESTION**
Would you spend a night on the Island of Dolls?

The Island of Dolls is the world's largest collection of haunted dolls. Over 4,000 dolls decorate the trees.

## LIVE ONCE, DIE TWICE

Día de los Muertos is an ancient festival in Mexico. Its traditions date back at least 3,000 years. It helps people remember the souls of the dead. If those spirits are forgotten, they are destroyed forever. The festival guides ghosts home to their living families. People set up altars with yummy foods. They decorate with bright flowers. People honor the dead in other ways too. For instance, they paint their faces to look like skulls. They make sugar candies that also resemble skulls.

# MYTHICAL ANIMAL GHOSTS AND SHAPESHIFTERS FROM AROUND THE WORLD

**DEER WOMAN** – known among the Ponca people of Nebraska; deer's head and legs; dressed like a woman in a veil; searches for her lost love

**SKIN-WALKER** – known among the Navajo of New Mexico and Arizona; a shapeshifter with glowing eyes that becomes many creatures, including coyotes; are the spirits of healers, known as medicine men or women, who turn evil

**WENDIGO** – a bony, owl-like spirit that has the power to make people crave human flesh, according to the indigenous tribes of the U.S. Great Lakes region and central Canada

**THE BLACK DOG (HELLHOUND)** – for thousands of years, people in England have reported seeing this ghost figure; it warns of death or tragedy

**LEMURS** – the Malagasy people of Madagascar believe lemurs are the spirits of their ancestors; the word "lemure" is Latin for "ghost"

**JAGUAR** – a spirit animal that travels between the world of the living and the dead; myths found on ruins across Central and South America

**SNOW LEOPARD** – this "ghost cat" is believed to be a shapeshifting mountain spirit across Central Asia because it seems to disappear before your eyes

**DUPPY** – a trickster ghost known in West Africa and the Caribbean islands; takes the form of birds, snakes, and lizards

# IN THE FORBIDDEN FOREST

*Hoia Baciu Forest is named for a shepherd who went missing there.*

The campers set up their tents. It was late day. The Hoia Baciu Forest was already dark. Crooked trees blocked the sun. The murky fog never thinned. No birds chirped. Nearby a twig snapped. The campers scanned the area. Would they see the shadow people? Those dark **specters** with glowing eyes. What about vampires? Or werewolves? This was Transylvania, after all.

Night fell. Pitch black smudged the woods. The campers huddled in their tent in the silent forest. Just as sleep pressed down, they heard it. *Thud*. A footstep.

Vampires are bodies without souls. Ghosts are souls without bodies. They are close mythical cousins.

## FREAKY FACT

The famous vampire novel *Dracula* was set not far from the Hoia Baciu Forest. It was based on legends about Prince Vlad III, a real-life person.

   More footsteps crunch nearby. The campers switch on headlamps. They peek outside the tent. The noises stop, but the campers see nothing. They sleep very little. Eventually, they break camp and leave before dawn.

Hoia Baciu has always been strange. Legend states a shepherd went missing there. So did his 200 sheep. Their bodies were never found. In another legend, a little girl went for a walk. She disappeared in the woods and was found five years later, wearing the same clothing. Mysteriously, she had not aged. She thought she'd been gone a few minutes.

## FREAKY FACT

Researchers found an ancient village under Hoia Baciu. Some people believe the spirits of the villagers haunt the forest.

Strange lights. UFO sightings. Bizarre trees with warped and twisted trunks. Some visitors report getting headaches, upset stomach, or rashes. They lose time like the little girl. The forest is home to many **supernatural** mysteries.

**Skeptics** say each mystery has a natural explanation. The forest is thick and trees twist to reach sunlight. Wildlife creates the shadow figures. The lights and UFOs result from an airport nearby. But legends are made to help people survive. For example, it is not safe to wander through forests alone.

# CAN GHOSTS GO EXTINCT?

When animals go extinct, they die off and no longer exist. Can this happen to ghosts? It might have. Old legends used to describe fiery ghosts, or Will-of-the-Wisps. These blue or green specters swooshed around swampy forests. Weirdly, these flaming ghosts were cold to the touch. Wisps are not really ghosts. They form when swamp gases ignite. Sadly, wisps are disappearing. As towns and cities grow, swamps and bogs shrink.

## CREEPY QUESTION

Some legends teach people helpful lessons. Can you think of a legend that is harmful instead of helpful?

# HAUNTED ROAD TRIP U.S.A.

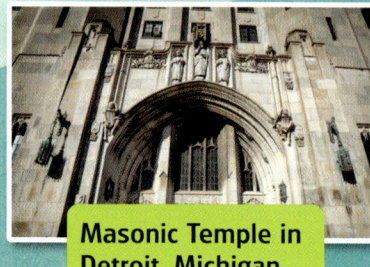
Masonic Temple in Detroit, Michigan

The Pittock Mansion in Portland, Oregon

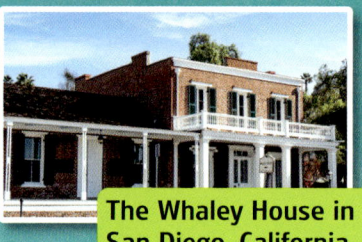
The Whaley House in San Diego, California

Hotel Monte Vista in Flagstaff, Arizona

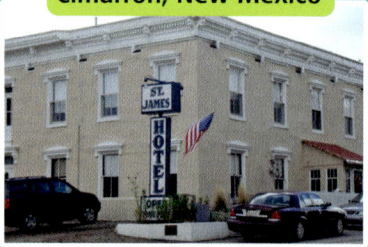
St. James Hotel in Cimarron, New Mexico

Ohio University in Athens, Ohio

Gettysburg National Park in Pennsylvania

Washington Irving Grave in Sleepy Hollow, New York

Trans-Allegheny Lunatic Asylum in Weston, West Virginia

Myrtles Plantation in Saint Francisville, Louisiana

Old City Jail in Charleston, South Carolina

# A DEADLY RIDE

*Spooky stories about **hitchhikers** who mysteriously vanish are common around the world.*

Anton La Grange drove deep into the night. The N9 highway cut through a desert in southern Africa. His headlights scraped over thorny bushes. They looked like shaggy beasts. Up ahead, Anton saw a hitchhiker. She had dark hair and wore nice pants and a coat. Anton did not want to leave her alone in the dark. He pulled over.

The woman opened the car door and sat in the front passenger seat. She gave Anton the address of her destination. They drove in silence. The lights of a town appeared. Anton turned to the woman, but she was gone. She had disappeared.

### FREAKY FACT

Vanishing hitchhikers are thought to be a special kind of ghost. They appear to be fully alive. Also, they can talk and tell stories.

Anton was spooked. He stopped at the police station and reported the mystery to an officer. "You are sleepy," the officer said. "Most likely you imagined it." Anton agreed and left. A few miles down the road, a woman's scream burst into his ears. He returned to the police station.

"I will drive behind you for a while. Until you feel safe," the officer said. They took off. By the time they were far from town, something strange happened. They drove through a mist. Suddenly, both Anton and the officer saw the passenger door of Anton's car open and close. Had an invisible person left the car?

## FREAKY FACT

Most vanishing hitchhiker stories are **urban legends**. These stories spread fast from person to person. They are usually not true.

The weird event shook the officer's memory. He returned to the station and pulled an old case file. It was for a car crash that happened many years ago. A woman named Maria Roux had died. He showed Anton her picture. "That's the woman I saw!" Anton said.

Besides meeting a ghost, what are some other good reasons to not pick up a hitchhiker?

Spotting an urban legend is easy. The basic story is always the same. Only the places and names are different. Anton's story may not be an urban legend because it can be traced to actual people and events. That is not true for most urban legends.

Many drivers on the N9 saw Maria's ghost for a decade. Locals claimed that Maria appeared once every year. A motorcyclist gave her a ride one night. Again, she disappeared. A married couple saw her. They pulled over and offered her a ride, which she accepted. Then she disappeared. Maria has not been seen again since 1984. Maybe she reached her final destination.

Experts estimate that about 109 billion people have lived and died on Earth. No wonder grave sites are so common.

## DIGGING UP THE TRUTH

Odds are good you have heard a ghost story about a place that is cursed because it was built on an ancient burial ground. Why are these stories so common? In some cases, these stories are urban legends. But there are plenty of true stories too. Lincoln Park in Chicago, Illinois, was built on graves dating back to the 1840s. New subway lines have cut through old grave sites. Workers building new homes uncover old graves. Old coffins have been found under many school playgrounds. Maybe dig with caution in your school's sandbox.

After reading the book, it's time to think about what you learned. Try the following exercises to jumpstart your ideas.

## THINK

**FIND OUT MORE.** Feeling haunted by ghostly myths and legends? There is so much more to discover. What else do you want to know? Ask your librarian for help finding the best books on supernatural myths. Visit a local museum and ask to hear the ghost stories they have tracked over time. Check with your family. What are the myths or legends that have been handed down over generations? Where do these tales come from?

## CREATE

**TIME FOR SOME ART.** What is your favorite ghostly myth or legend? Now imagine you are going to make a movie about this story. Create a movie poster. Use images to explain what the movie is about. Draw a detailed picture of the ghosts or spirits involved. Are they spooky or friendly? Are they helpful or hurtful?

## SHARE

**THE MORE WHO KNOW.** Share what you learned from this book about ghostly myths and legends. Use your own words to create an idea board. Write down the main ideas of this book. Pin them to the board. What facts from the book support these main ideas? Pin them to the board. Share your idea board with a classmate. Pin their questions or comments to the board.

## GROW

**HELPING HANDS.** All the myths and legends in this book have one thing in common. They are all invitations to explore. Research about death and dying. Interview your classmates and your teachers. What do they believe happens when a person dies? Do they believe in spirits of the dead? Why or why not? Listen. Take notes. Be respectful. Beliefs are sacred to us all.

# RESEARCH NINJA

Visit www.ninjaresearcher.com/8383 to learn how to take your research skills and book report writing to the next level!

## Research

**DIGITAL LITERACY TOOLS**

### SEARCH LIKE A PRO
Learn how to use search engines to find useful websites.

### FACT OR FAKE
Discover how you can tell a trusted website from an untrustworthy resource.

### TEXT DETECTIVE
Explore how to zero in on the information you need most.

### SHOW YOUR WORK
Research responsibly—learn how to cite sources.

## Write

**DOWNLOADABLE BOOK REPORT FORMS**

### GET TO THE POINT
Learn how to express your main ideas.

### PLAN OF ATTACK
Learn prewriting exercises and create an outline.

# Further Resources

## BOOKS

Boardman, Adam Allsuch. *An Illustrated History of Ghosts*. London: Nobrow, 2022.

Deyoe, Aaron. *Biggest, Baddest Book of Ghosts*. Minneapolis, MN: ABDO, 2015.

Fitzpatrick, Insha. *Chilling with Ghosts: A Totally Factual Field Guide to the Supernatural*. Philadelphia, PA: Quirk Books, 2023.

## WEBSITES

Factsurfer.com gives you a safe, fun way to find more information.

1. Go to www.factsurfer.com.
2. Enter "Spine-Chilling Legends and Myths" into the search box and click 🔍.
3. Select your book cover to see a list of related websites.

# GLOSSARY

**coffins:** Boxes into which dead people are placed for burial.

**hitchhikers:** People who travel by getting rides in other people's vehicles, usually by standing on the side of the road and holding up the thumb as a signal to stop.

**ignite:** To set fire to something or to catch fire.

**legends:** Stories handed down from the past that are usually based on facts or actual events.

**myths:** Old stories that express the beliefs or history of a group of people, or that explain some natural event.

**ritual:** An ancient series of acts that are always performed in the same way, usually as part of a religious or social ceremony.

**skeptics:** People who do not accept views or opinions readily from others.

**specters:** Ghosts or phantoms that are usually unpleasant or threatening.

**supernatural:** Existing outside normal human experience or knowledge.

**urban legends:** Scary or funny stories that are presented as truth, but which are usually false.

# INDEX

Barrera, Don Julian Santana, 7, 8, 9, 10
Dia de los Muertos, 11
Dracula, 15
forests, 5, 14, 15, 17, 18, 19
ghosts, 4, 5, 7, 9, 11, 12, 13, 15, 19, 23, 25, 26
haunted, 5, 7, 9, 10, 17, 20
haunted dolls, 5, 6, 7, 10
haunted sites map, 20, 21
highway ghosts, 5, 22
hitchhikers, 22, 23, 24, 25
Hoia Baciu Forest, 14, 15, 17, 18
Island of Dolls, 5, 6, 7, 8, 9, 10
legends, 5, 15, 17, 18, 19, 24, 25, 27
noises, 7, 14, 15, 16, 24
shadow figures, 14, 18
shapeshifters, 12, 13
souls, 11, 15
spirits, 4, 9, 10, 11, 12, 13, 17
Transylvania, 14, 15
urban legends, 24, 25, 27
vampires, 14, 15
vanishing, 22, 23, 24, 26
whispers, 6, 9, 10

## PHOTO CREDITS

The images in this book are reproduced through the courtesy of: iobard (sea serpent), Color Brush (branch)/Shutterstock Images, cover; RAY-BON/Shutterstock Images, p.4; Creativa Images/Shutterstock Images, p.5; Esparta Palma/Wikimedia Commons, p.6; HammadKhn/Shutterstock Images, p.7; marketa1982/Shutterstock Images, p.7; CassielMx/Shutterstock Images, p.7; marketa1982/Shutterstock Images, p.8; Maroyen Design/Shutterstock Images, p.9; marketa1982/Shutterstock Images, p.10; Moab Republic/Shutterstock Images, p.11; Fer Gregory/Shutterstock Images, p.11 (circle); Nejron Photo/Shutterstock Images, p.12; Aden kowalski/Wikimedia Commons, p.12; Jakubdrastich2/Wikimedia Commons, p.12; Daniel Eskridge/Shutterstock Images, p.13 (top left); yakub88/Shutterstock Images, p.13 (top right); Einstock/Shutterstock Images, p.13 (middle left); Abeselom Zerit/Shutterstock Images, p.13 (middle right); GoodFocused/Shutterstock Images, p.13 (bottom); Daniel Marian/Shutterstock Images, p.14; Robcartorres/Shutterstock Images, p.15 (book); Bardocz Peter/Shutterstock Images, p.15; Aaron Cabral/Shutterstock Images, p.16; Hywit Dimyadi/Shutterstock Images, p.16 (footprint); thsulemani/Shutterstock Images, p.17; WesAbrams/iStock, p.18 (flying saucer); Paul Horia Malaianu/Shutterstock Images, p.18; AvDi/Shutterstock Images, p.19; Belikova Oksana/Shutterstock Images, p.20 (top right); Png Studio Photography/Shutterstock Images, p.20 (top left); Sherry V Smith/Shutterstock Images, p.20 (middle); Framalicious/Shutterstock Images, p.20 (bottom left); PhotoTrippingAmerica/Shutterstock Images, p.20 (bottom right); Ken Wolter/Shutterstock Images, p.21 (top left); James Kirkikis/Shutterstock Images, p.21 (top right); Paul Juser/Shutterstock Images, p.21 (middle first); Malachi Jacobs/Shutterstock Images, p.21 (middle second); Sonicpuss/Shutterstock Images, p.21 (bottom right); Nina Alizada/Shutterstock Images, p.21 (bottom left); Venn-Photo/Shutterstock Images, p.22; Virrage Images/Shutterstock Images, p.23; Raggedstone/Shutterstock Images, p.24; J.Thasit/Shutterstock Images, p.25; Castleski/Shutterstock Images, p.25 (stamp); hidesy/Shutterstock Images, p.26 (sign); Krivosheev Vitaly/Shutterstock Images, p.26; Jacob Karmel/Shutterstock Images, p.27.

## ABOUT THE AUTHOR

Jenny Mason grew up in a haunted town where spookiness roamed wild. No wonder Jenny is a scary story hunter today. She explores foreign countries, canyon mazes, and burial crypts to gather the facts that make the truest (and scariest) tales. She received an MFA in Writing for Children and Young Adults from the Vermont College of Fine Arts. She also holds an MPhil from Trinity College Dublin.